D1435180

PLAIN
CHINGLISH

Oliver Lutz Radtke

WITHDRAWN

GIBBS SMITH
TO ENRICH AND INSPIRE HUMANKIND

First Edition
23 22 21 20 19   5 4 3 2 1

Published by
Gibbs Smith
P.O. Box 667
Layton, Utah 84041

1.800.835.4993 orders
www.gibbs-smith.com

Designed by Fran Lee

Gibbs Smith books are printed on paper produced from sustainable
PEFC-certified forest/controlled wood source. Learn more at www.pefc.org.
Printed and bound in Hong Kong

Library of Congress Control Number: 2018966887
ISBN: 978-1-4236-5265-6

This book is dedicated to
my grandmother

Irmgard Radtke

(1924–2018).
I miss her laughter.

Beijing (2011)

CONTENTS

· ·

Introduction   1

Interview with Professor David Moser   5

Notices and Reminders   9

Public Services   27

Public Education   37

Tourism   51

Directions   59

Menus   69

Commercials and Products   81

In Praise of Chinglish   100

Photo Credits   104

Acknowledgments   105

豪华尊贵的盛会 名流云集的家园
Luxury home valued event celebrity **studded**

贵宾热线: 0470-8252222

开启全景生活 展现全新人生
Open the panoramic life to **show** a new life

贵宾热线: 0470-8252222

繁华与宁静共存，阔绰身份不显自露
The prosperous and peaceful coexistence, rich identity not **significant** since the **dew**

贵宾热线: 0470-8252222

365天的贴身护卫，阔度管理以您为尊
365 days of the bodyguard, width of management in **your hand**

贵宾热线: 0470-8252222

Hohot (2012)

INTRODUCTION

"The prosperous and peaceful coexistence, rich identity not significant since the dew," screams the real estate billboard in Hohhot, the capital of China's Inner Mongolia Autonomous Region, in big brown letters. What it actually wants to say is that the property on sale combines proximity to the city center while still providing quiet, and because of its understated design your wealth won't show (an aspect favored by many Chinese millionaires). With a smile, I reach for my cell phone to document the sign as I have done for almost twenty years while working and traveling in China.

My fascination with Chinglish goes back to the year 2000, when you would find me as a Chinese studies major in Shanghai wandering wide-eyed about the Huangpu river metropolis, jotting down new Chinglish observations in a notebook—no smartphones back then—and trying to understand a new universe of words and ways to use them.

Chinglish, publicly accessible English translations (often confused with Chinese grammar) was everywhere. The country was about to join the World Trade Organization (WTO) and was in the middle of a bidding process for the 2008 Summer Olympic Games—bilingual hilarities started to pop up everywhere. I felt privileged to witness this blossoming period of Chinglish firsthand and to see how the English language, or its unconsciously creative interpretations, visibly crept into the linguistic landscape of the city.

But why would I as a German native undertake this mission to document and explain Chinglish signs all over the country? Since I am neither an English nor a Chinese native speaker I am blessed to observe the application of both languages from a third culture vantage point, much less influenced by their traditions and conventions. I am equally curious about English as I am about Chinese and a humble learner of both, which has awarded me with the rare opportunity of immersing myself into two very different linguistic universes. Additionally, as the son of a retired proofreader, I was surely destined by family tradition to take a closer look at writing in the first place!

When I compiled the first volume of *Chinglish* ten years ago, things had already changed visibly from the days of my early Shanghai observations. I lived in Beijing, which was gearing up an impressive amount of (mostly student) manpower to eradicate Chinglish from the capital with the stated goal of getting rid of it nationwide. Fast forward ten years later and it is safe to say that the powers in place have been successful in cleaning up a lot. First-tier cities such as Beijing and Shanghai look very neat—some observers call it dull—an indicator of the increased administrative efficiency and raised awareness for better translation quality. But leave the metropoles and Chinglish hits you right in the face again, and will continue to do so in second- and third-tier cities like Changchun, Fuzhou, or Guiyang (not to mention the hundreds of fourth-tier ones) for many years to come. Chinglish is here to stay.

Defining Chinglish

Chinglish can be viewed as a spoken and written phenomenon. The former is an oral hybrid during second language acquisition or a creative blend by second-generation Chinese growing up using both languages. This is an established academic field, also looking at the emergence of Kongish, a conscious language choice in Hong Kong to strengthen local identity.

Chinglish in this book deals with bilingual public signage and items with written interpretations of English. With the following pages, I invite you to understand that Chinglish can be more than just a quirky mix of an English dictionary and Chinese grammar.

Chinglish is firstly a by-product of China's sincere efforts toward modernization. It embodies the country's linguistic contact zone with the world. Chinglish is a laudable attempt by the state and the market to cater to a non-Chinese speaking audience, accommodating foreigners in the world's lingua franca. However, even if resources are available, the sign maker's awareness for high-quality translation is still oftentimes low, and the intended bilingual message results in a grandiose crash landing. With this book, I am in part certainly aiming to criticize official and non-official entities that should know better and just do not care where care is due, especially in critical areas such as hospitals, airports, allergy indications on product labels and menus, and so on. But, even more so, I want to express my appreciation to individuals, organizations, and enterprises that try to cater to an international audience and do it, consciously or not, in a different way than native speakers would normally have it, making you smile and ponder a message that you might have ignored otherwise.

The main producers of Chinglish are the state and the market. State Chinglish comes in the form of mostly anonymous communication with the general public, consisting of (less friendly) notices and (very friendly) reminders. Both revolve around public services, directions, tourism, and public education. The latter strikes a non-Chinese reader as an unusual form of state communication in highlighting a rather paternalistic attitude towards its citizens. On the one hand, this shows a form of official care, reminding its citizens not to spit everywhere in order to avoid spreading infections and so on. On the other hand, the state acts as the creator and reminder of "civilized" behavior, with many Chinese privately objecting to this form of authority. Furthermore, the official party language, an already highly complex set of codes and expressions in Chinese, makes it almost impossible to find non-clumsy sounding equivalents in English.

While state signs have improved a lot, the market economy provides the real soil for Chinglish flowers to blossom: on shop signs, in commercials, and on products—especially stationery and clothes. The latter two have shed Chinese characters altogether, suggesting that English here is used as a form of projected cosmopolitanism with an exclusively domestic audience in mind, similar to Kanji sweaters or Chinese character tattoos in the West. The biggest Chinglish provider these days is certainly the restaurant menu. Chinese dish names are particularly rich with historical analogies, flowery imagery, and puns that will hardly ever cease to provide opportunities for Chinglish results, especially when relying on free online translation software.

What Chinglish says about us

Part of the motivation that keeps me going is how Chinglish continuously challenges our linguistic conventions. A "deformed person toilet" in Kunming or the "Anus Hospital" in Beijing are funny because they instantly destroy euphemisms we have carefully built up—in the medical world mostly through Latin terms—when talking about sensitive topics. Chinglish annihilates these conventions and I learn from it as much about foreign tongues as I learn about my own. Chinglish is almost always an invitation to explore our own mind-set and a unique chance to engage in humorous dialogue with Chinese speakers.

The future of Chinglish

With forty years of establishing US-People's Republic of China diplomatic relations, it is safe to say that we still have a lot to learn. Chinglish is but one small, humorous platform to contribute to that task. With the era of artificial intelligence dawning on us, the translation trade seems to be more in the hands of algorithms than ever. Language created by humans, its poetry and depth, its cleverness and beauty, needs, at least at some point, the touch of a human translator. We do not seek mathematical correctness; instead, what we need as humans is understanding, smiles, and an emotional connection, which comes first and foremost through language.

Languages are fluid and constantly evolving, and the world is moving toward more hybridization every day. Cultures and languages have been interacting and influencing each other for millennia. If languages like cultures resist change, they fossilize and face extinction. Longevity goes hand in hand with creativity. The richness of the English language— more than one million words and counting—comes from the fact that it is open to foreign influences, and Chinglish will continue to be an influence as well. If the language we use daily has such an open attitude, we should have an open attitude, too.

Interview with PROFESSOR DAVID MOSER

An interview with Professor David Moser, Associate Dean of Yenching Academy of Peking University, and author of *A Billion Voices: China's Search for a Common Language*.

David, what is Chinglish for you?

Chinglish is a delightful cross-linguistic entanglement that results in an amusing—and sometimes disastrous—confusion of form and content.

What do you mean by that?

The linguistic shock of a piece of Chinglish is somewhat similar to that of a pun or a beautiful turn of phrase in a poem. It makes us aware of the complex swirl of meaning that surrounds every word and phrase in the language—a semantic mix that we are often unaware of. Chinglish is almost never an arbitrary or random mishap; there is often a deeper reason for the confusion that has to do with the wonderful complexity of semantics and context.

Looking at Chinglish, for me, is fascinating because I have almost always something new to discover about my own linguistic habits and presumptions, not to mention a ton of things to learn about why certain expressions were used. For you, why is looking at Chinglish more than a cheap joke?

As a translator, I take Chinglish very seriously. Chinglish is instructive because it reveals the unexpected ways in which foreign languages can present us with unexpected pitfalls. We laugh at Chinglish for the reason we laugh at ordinary bad translations. Chinglish is just a bad translation that becomes high art by virtue of its spectacular failure. It is like the pleasure of watching a truly awful movie: it makes us laugh, but it also allows us to see the process of incredible complexity and craft that is often made invisible by more skilled artisans.

You arrived in China in 1987. What was the status of Chinglish back then?

This was a Golden Age of Chinglish, you might say. Confronted with an influx of foreigners, municipalities and work units had the task of translating a huge amount of public information and tourist signage into English. Most of the officials in charge of this task knew little or no English, and were blissfully unaware of the difficulties of quality translation. Therefore the duty of translating fell on the shoulders of low-level office personnel who had at least a modicum of English language ability. English was a required course in most schools, but few people had even had a chance to try out their English with a foreigner, much less to actually go abroad to live and work in an English-language environment. Thus these hapless translators, having virtually no access to native English speakers to check the results of their efforts, produced vast quantities of hilariously bad English that simply slipped by unnoticed.

The importance and presence of English as a foreign language has grown enormously since then. China has joined the WTO, holds international prestige events, such as the 2008 Summer Olympic Games, 2010 Expo Shanghai China, Asia-Pacific Economic Cooperation (APEC), and so on. Why is Chinglish nevertheless still out there?

It's an endangered species, for sure, but it's still there. Chinglish is still being produced because the powers that be still aren't willing to muster the resources it would take to eradicate it. The folks who control budgets are usually the least likely to care about elegant translation and linguistic accuracy. Bless their hearts.

I am still, after twenty years, astonished at the incredibly confident display of unchecked translations on public signs. Sometimes I envy the city officials' thick skins! With official China's new "going out" policy and telling the world how it really is, why is the awareness for good translation still so low?

I've often felt the same way. I've worked in State media and Chinese companies long enough to realize that part of the reason Chinglish persists has to do with saving face. When participating in a project involving translation issues, I would often point out to the supervisor that the translation should be checked by me or other native speakers. My warnings would often be waved off with reassurances like "No need for that, don't worry! We have Xiao Wang here, who spent a year in London; her English is perfect." While some colleagues in the office—and even Xiao Wang herself—might suspect that the final outcome was less than "perfect English," who is going to be so heartless as to cause Xiao Wang to lose face—and her job—by challenging the quality of the translation?

How long will Chinglish survive? With China's massive investment in artificial intelligence, do you foresee a time when machine translation will actually reach human capabilities? I cannot imagine with Chinese—a language blessed with such rich imagery and historical anecdotes—that the human brain can ever be fully taken out of the equation.

Chinglish will survive as long as there are linguistic and cultural differences between us. To the extent that "vive la difference" is an inspiration slogan, we should hope that it survives for the near future. As for machine translation, ironically some of the best (worst?) examples these days are due precisely to the lazy reliance on translation software. Machine translation is still far from being able to adequately translate signage, precisely because such language use always involves subtle aspects of tone, register, and culture backgrounding that remain stubbornly impossible to automate. I agree completely with you; quality translation will probably always require the participation of human beings who have lived in and experienced the language and culture.

How is Chinglish useful for improving intercultural communication?

In a way, it is useful as a counter-example. As I mentioned, bad movies are instructive examples of how not to make movies, and Chinglish provides us endless—and endlessly entertaining—examples of how not to do translation.

I am worried that large-scale rectification campaigns focus on standardizing translations to an extent that non-Chinese speakers lose access to the flowery beauty of the language. Do you share this worry or do we just have to move to smaller cities to keep enjoying these?

I agree that part of joy of such translations is that it presents the English-speaking foreigner with a wonderful window onto the cultural "flavor" and rhetorical richness of Chinese. But I wouldn't worry about this aspect disappearing completely. The signage departments may become alerted to these supposedly face-losing translations and standardize all future occurrences, but humanity is constantly evolving, with new technologies, new customs, and new public realities, all of which will necessitate new translation solutions.

Is there anything that Chinglish can contribute to in the field of understanding contemporary China better?
Chinglish has been prevalent because of the importance of English as the world's lingua franca. As Chinese becomes more important, we're starting to see the emergence of "Englese" or whatever the opposite phenomenon should be called. When native speakers of English start being forced to produce signs in Chinese, I predict the next Oliver Lutz Radtke will be Chinese, and he or she will be collecting hilarious examples of how Chinese is butchered by hapless non-Chinese translators.

I look forward to that! Many thanks, David!

NOTICES
AND
REMINDERS

State or non-state notices are usually serious business: things you have to know, orders you have to follow, behavior that is forbidden. Their layout is usually either text-heavy or very short and the tone is formal and strict. Reminders—also the ones issued by state actors such as police—come rather light-handed with cartoon faces and sweet vocabulary. Many reminder signs alert you to *zhuyi* (pay attention) to safety or be generally *xiao xin* (cautious), often about your head or variations of that body part. Corporate management signs have replaced a lot of caution signs previously issued by the state, highlighting the continuing trend of commercialization of public space.

Beijing (2018)

Suzhou (2016)

Sanya (2017)

RIGHT: The Chinese original means "Be careful of falling rocks." Where does "the truth" come from? There is a Chinese proverb with exactly these two characters in the middle: *shui luo shi chu.* "When the water subsides, the rocks emerge," which means "the truth comes to light." Maybe the machine translation was slightly influenced by its Buddhist surroundings, who knows?

Yungang Grottoes, Datong (2018)

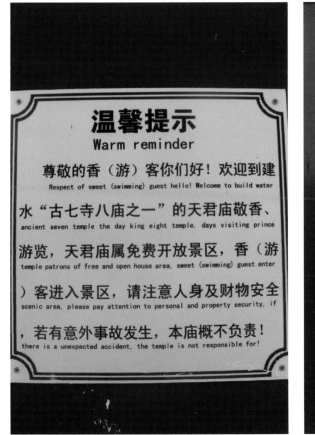

温馨提示
Warm reminder

尊敬的香（游）客你们好！欢迎到建
Respect of sweet (swimming) guest hello! Welcome to build water

水"古七寺八庙之一"的天君庙敬香、
ancient seven temple the day king eight temple, days visiting prince

游览，天君庙属免费开放景区，香（游
temple patrons of free and open house area, sweet (swimming) guest enter

）客进入景区，请注意人身及财物安全
scenic area, please pay attention to personal and property security, if

，若有意外事故发生，本庙概不负责！
there is a unexpected accident, the temple is not responsible for!

Jianshui (2013)

温馨提示
Just so you know

尊敬的居民及朋友们：

● 为了保障胡同内居民的正常生活秩序；

● 请朋友们进入胡同时爱护环境，

　勿进入私人宅院；

● 禁止流动商贩等进入胡同；

● 请机动车辆配合登记工作。

安定门街道办事处
东旭佳业物业管理有限责任公司

Beijing (2018)

Beijing (2016)

Huzhou (2017)

ABOVE AND RIGHT: *Xiao xin*: "Careful," literally, "small heart," is a wonderful example of the ambiguity of the Chinese language. In the original it can mean both "be careful" or "carefully." Be careful of the slippery floor or carefully slip? An impossible task for machine translations!

Beijing (2018)

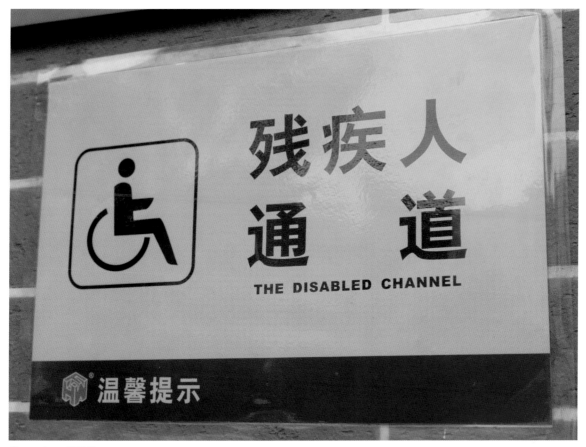

残疾人
通　道
THE DISABLED CHANNEL

温馨提示

Guangzhou (2011)

设备故障

The facility does not work
because of its malfunction

Shanghai (2017)

Beijing (2018)

Shanghai (2016)

Beijing (2011)

Beijing (2016)

禁止大便

Due to the issue of flush away, please do not Poo, thanks.

警方提示
POLICE REMINDS

不要打架
FIGHT IS PROHIBITED

打输住院
IF YOU LOSE YOU WILL BE HOSPITALIZED

打赢坐牢
IF YOU WIN YOU WILL GO TO JAIL

打架成本高 下手需谨慎

1. 轻微伤打架直接成本＝5日至15日拘留＋500至1000元罚款＋医药费＋误工费等赔偿＋因拘留少挣的工资。
2. 轻伤的打架直接成本＝3年以下有期徒刑＋赔偿金＋医药费＋误工费等赔偿＋因拘留少挣的工资＋悔恨的泪水。
3. 重伤的打架等直接成本＝3年以上10年以下有期徒刑、无期徒刑或死刑＋经济赔偿＋社会及家庭严重影响。
4. 打架的附加成本：民事责任费用（诉讼费＋律师费＋医药费＋误工费）公安机关酿料劣迹＋心情沮丧郁闷＋名誉形象受损＋家人朋友困扰＋工作生意等遭受更大的损失。

派出所报警电话：
021-59598110

派出所全天不打烊 但请您最好别光顾
嘉定公安分局黄渡派出所

Shanghai (2018)

Shanghai (2018)

水深危险　禁止游泳
THE DEPTH OF DANGER NO SWIMMING

Nanjing (2018)

三、严禁运送超长、超高、超重及危险物品。

ATTENTION

1. Passengers should hold the handrail band, face the moving direction, and move away the feet from the stage margin.
2. Take the escalator politely; The older, the children, the deformities, the patients and the pregnant women should take the escalator with his guardian together.
3. The too longer, too higher, overweight and the dangerous things are not allowed to be carried.

Beijing (2010)

停车须知
Notice

1、仅供本饭店消费的宾客免费停车
Freedom for the quests in our hotel

2、请将车辆停放整齐、锁好车门
Please stop the car in line and lock the door

3、请勿将贵重物品留置车内，以防失窃
Please don't leave the valuable in the car

未按停车须知操作，如有损失本饭店不承担任何责任。
If you dont follow parking rules, causing the cars or valuadle things lost, the hotle has no duty!

Nanjing (2018)

Quzhou (2008)

花开堪赏直须赏
莫要折花空赏枝
Plants Also Have Lives.
No Picking.

Zhangye (2018)

Changchun (2018)

温馨提示

请将卫生用品投入垃圾桶
Please put health supplies into trash can

马桶不是大胃王！
The toilet is not a big stomach king!

吞了异物会抓狂
Swallowed foreign body will be mad

Shanghai (2017)

Shenzhen (2018)

Yunnan (2014)

Suzhou (2018)

定桌接待单位

非入住者
请勿进

Do not enter non-residents

Pingyao (2009)

請勿吐痰
No spitting

嚴禁擺放雜物
No paraphernalia

請勿在椅上躺臥
No lying on benches

Chengdu (2012)

谢绝参观，请勿打扰

Politely refuse visiting , and please don't disturb

Suzhou (2016)

施工现场
请您注意安全
Construction under Way
Please Stay Away.

Chengdu (2011)

PUBLIC SERVICES

Many public services in China, including fire stations, mobile police stations, trash cans, traffic, and construction signs are bilingual. That is quite an accomplishment for such a huge country and again shows that a lack of resources is often not the cause for Chinglish, but rather still very low translation awareness.

Nanjing (2018)

满　意　出　入　境

SATISFIED WITH THE ENTRY AND EXIT

Nanjing (2017)

Guangzhou (2010)

手机加油站

HANDSET GAS STATION

旅客自弃物品箱
Voluntarily Abandoned Items

旅客火机火柴自弃箱

桂林两江国际机场安全检查站

Pingyao (2009)

休 息 茶 室
The rest of the teahouse
旅 行 超 市
Travel supermarket

小 件 寄 存
Left Luggage

Dali (2018)

PUBLIC EDUCATION

Under the realm of public education falls everything ranging from state propaganda about "socialist core values" and the "China Dream" to reminders of citizen responsibilities and proper public behavior. For a foreign traveler ubiquitous reminders to behave in a certain way may come across as an unusual form of communication and may strike us as rather paternalistic. On top, certain concepts are just hard to translate. A prime example is *wenming* which literally means "civilization" or "civilized" (Chinese nouns can also be adjectives) but is also used to propagate a wide range of concepts such as "civility," "civic responsibility," and "politeness." Public education heavily relies on all aspects of *wenming* to educate the population on so-called civilized behavior, and on environmentally conscious and hygienic behavior. Especially in public parks, at tourist sites, and in restrooms one finds a lot of creative signs trying to raise awareness for the beauty of unplucked flower beds, or for visiting sites and museums in a non-hooligan way. Quite a few Chinese express privately that the state should be less concerned with telling them what civilized behavior means and focus more on key tasks such as an affordable social security system.

向前一小步
A Small Step forward
文明一大步
A Big Stride for Civilization

Shanghai (2016)

BELOW: Many public park signs in China feature poetic couplets with four characters in two lines and a rhyme scheme, a form that dates back to the Book of Songs *(Shi jing),* one of the Five Classics traditionally said to be compiled by Confucius himself. *Xiao cao qing qing, jiao xia liu qing:* "The tiny grass is green, show mercy with your feet."

出游莫忘文明
购物还须理性

Civilized behavior of tourists is another
bright scenery rational shopping

Heshun (2013)

Suzhou (2016)

Beijing (2011)

众人携手保平安

All of us should contribute oursevles to the security of the great

Beijing (2010)

请勿在便池
内乱扔纸屑

Please don't in the urina throwing confetti

Beijing (2016

贴近文明 靠近方便

Closer, Easier

Beijing (2009)

贴近文明　靠近方便

Keep close to the civilization , near the convenience

Inner Mongolia (2012)

44

Kunming (2016)

这是我一直想对你说的话：
This is what I've always wanted to talk to you!

共建文明公厕　共享健康生活
Build civilized public lavatory　Enjoy healthy life

节约用水　文明你最美
Saving water　you are the best ...

小便入池　文明你最美
Urinating into the pool　you are the best ...

及时冲水　文明你最美
Flushing timely　you are the best ...

爱护公物　文明你最美
Protecting public property　you are the best ...

讲文明更健康
BE CIVIL BE HEALTHY

首都精神文明建设委员会办公室
OFFICE OF BEIJING CIVIC ENHANCEMENT COMMITTEE
北京市市政市容管理委员会
BEIJING MUNICIPAL COMMISSION OF
CITY ADMINISTRATION AND ENVIRONMENT

旅途愉快

爱护环境
文明旅游
Protecting of our environment,
be the civilization tourism .

Beijing (2018)

Chengyang (2016)

Siguniangshan (2017)

Urumuqi (2016)

Inner Mongolia (2018)

Tianjin (2011)

留住花的美
体现你的美

Keep the beauty of flowers to show the beauty of your own

Inner Mongolia (2011)

Kunming (2016)

飞花触水

本是一片蛙鼓鸣奏的乡村水塘，如今成为酒吧环绕，游客徜徉的酒吧休闲区。若待四月楸木花开，春风荡漾之时，你便会看见无数花朵从半空中幸福地飞坠柔波里。或者，夜半酒酣，如花的美女也会飞身跳入池中，那是真正的飞花触水！

Flyings Tease Water

There used to be a district of country ponds filling with croaking, but now it becomes an area of all sorts of bars filling with tourists. Especially in April, with blossoming of Jiumu, you can see numbers of flyings falling into the water. Or else, with a little drunk at midnight, you can enjoyan even more exciting scene:numbers of beauties are flying into the water!

TOURISM

Tourism administrative bodies are rightfully proud of their beautiful heritage sites. The problem on site: China's history is long and visitors' time is short. Few people in charge have an idea of how to tell historical stories in a captivating way. The traditional approach is to drown visitors in facts and figures. A lot can be achieved by actually thinking first about what kind of story should be told. Often less is more.

情人洞
Lover hole

Outside Beijing (2015)

Huzhou (2015)

平遥文庙学宫 Pingyao Confucius Temple

早餐通道
Breakfast channel

景区出口
The scenic spot to export

Pingyao (2016)

全国文明风景旅游区　National Civilization Scenery Tourism Region

示　范　点

Example Spot

中央精神文明建设指导委员会办公室
中华人民共和国建设部
国　家　旅　游　局
一九九八年六月

The Office of Directing Committee of China Central Spiritual
Civilization Construction
The Construction Ministry of the People's Republic of China
National Tourism Administration

June ,1998

漓江风景游览线（叠彩山—阳朔）　Lijiang River Tourist Route (Diecai Hill-Yangshuo)

Guilin (2009)

Lijiang (2013)

Beijing (2011)

党史
PARTY OF THE HISTORY

Beijing (2010)

请在一米黄线外等候
Please wait outside the line in a beige

Chifeng (2017)

DIRECTIONS

China is big; visitors are often in need of directions. Impressively, many public and private signs offer some sort of bilingual help. But Baidu Translate (the equivalent to Google Translate) or Kingsoft just don't cut it yet, especially since directions are a very codified language to translate. Quite a few academic delegations travel frequently to the US and UK to study their public sign systems. These insights will slowly (and figuratively) translate into more standardization across the country. For some signs, this is a blessing, for others, it takes away the opportunity to smile.

60

人工售票处
Artificial Tickets

改签、退票
Ticket transfer&Return

公安制证点
ID Card Manufacture

（向前100米右侧下地道）

售票处
Ticket Office

Shanghai (2018)

LEFT: *Rengong shoupiao chu:* The first two characters (*rengong*) actually mean "artificial," as in "man-made" (not natural), but here it indicates a ticket office manned with an actual human selling tickets. Since *rengong zhineng* artificial intelligence is all the rage right now in China, maybe the online translation software that self-adjusts according to the demand for certain words automatically assumes these two characters can only mean artificial these days (which is true in many ways).

爱心专座

Love Special Seat

Guangzhou (2010)

Inner Mongolia (2014)

Guilin (2009)

ABOVE: Writing in China these days (newspapers, chats, blogs, love letters) is the same as in the West: from left to right. Traditionally, though, one would write from right to left. Nowadays this approach is used to convey a sense of poetic beauty or sophistication. Seeing this on a river cruise boat for tourists near Guilin was reason enough to chuckle. The most fascinating aspect, however, was to detect the English translation underneath written in the same fashion, from right to left. If Chinese characters can be written that way, why shouldn't it be done with English letters?

弯 道 减 速
Curve-speed plaque

Beijing (2016)

蛋白质 8.04（g）
脂肪 9.97（g）
碳水化合物 35.38（g）
膳食纤维 0.75（g）

¥**4**/个

羊肉稍麦
Mutton Is A Bit Of Wheat

¥**4**/个（4个起卖）【120】

营养成分表

项目	每100克
能量	217.88（kcal）
蛋白质	5.66（g）
脂肪	0.68（g）
碳水化合物	46.33（g）
膳食纤维	0.72（g）

西葫芦稍麦
Squash A Mic

¥**3**/个（4个起卖）【121】

MENUS

Chinese people are rightfully proud of their long culinary history and dish names are often as refined as their ingredients, rich with word plays that are impossible for any translation software to master. Since people want to eat every day, and restaurants won't go out of business in China, it is safe to say that even if all other Chinglish will have been corrected (already unlikely), menu Chinglish will always be there as long as people provide food and expect foreigners to show up as well. Menus alone are a wonderful reason to start learning Chinese. Not only to discover the clever puns but also because they taste even better if you order them in the chef's language.

lead a person to endless aftertastes

Share with your favorite people
香港·深圳·上海·合肥
分享給您最愛的人
Share with your favorite people

Huai'an (2018)

Chicken scratched in front of a piece of noodl

煎雞扒出前一丁麵 ★★

Fried chicken and rice noodles

煎雞扒米粉 ★★

A piece of noodles before frying the pork

煎豬扒出前一丁麵

Pork chop rice noodles

煎豬扒米粉

Dice of tomato beef before it comes out

濃湯番茄牛肉出前一丁

Tomato and beef rice noodles

濃湯番茄牛肉米粉

Huai'an (2018)

Huai'an (2018)

家常土豆丝
Often the potatoes

¥**22**/份【554】

午餐套餐

set lunch

星期一 Monday

A 玫瑰豉油鸡饭 45/例
Rose chicken rice

B 广东炒
Fried rice

C 剁椒鱼头腩钵仔饭 42/例
Chop the pretzel head, eat the rice.

D 招牌炒
Brand fried

星期二 Tuesday

台式炒飯
Desktop fried rice
デスクトップチャーハン

Yuchi Township, Taiwan (2017)

702
私家肉丸/例
¥48.00
◎ 译文 : Private meatballs

Beijing (2015)

青椒拆骨肉 ¥28
Green pepper demolition of the same flesh
and blood

豆角烧茄子是一道家常炒菜

12

色绝嗹美
ABSOLUTELY BEAUTIFUL

豆角含丰富维生素

Guangzhou (2018)

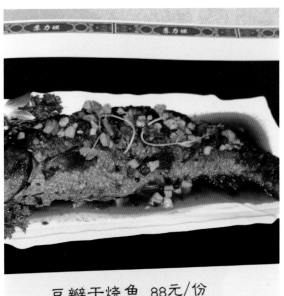

豆瓣干烧鱼 88元/份
Beans do burn fish
Фасоли горят рыб
الفول القيام بحرق الاساك

Beijing (2015)

75

菜 谱
仙峰小吃店价目表

菜 名	价 格
素菜、蕃茄、蛋炒饭 Vegetable dish Fried rice with egg and tomato	30 元/份
洋葱肉丝 The onion shredded meat	40 元/份
土豆肉丝 Potato shredded meat	40 元/份
回锅肉 Double cooked pork slices	45 元/份
竹笋肉 Bamboo shoot meat	40 元/份
青椒肉丝 Shredded pork and green pepper	40 元/份
木耳炒肉 The fungus fried meat	40 元/份
白菜炒肉 Fried meat with Chinese Cabbage	40 元/份
魔芋炒肉 Fried meat with fried meat	40 元/份
蕃茄炒蛋 Fried eggs with tomatoes	30 元/份
油炸土豆条 Fried potato chips	35 元/份
土豆丝　　Potato silk	25 元/份

096 烧全素

Burn all the meat

RMB: 16 元/例

Emei Shan (2018)

Shanghai (2015)

BELOW: This is a wonderful example of what happens when machine translation does its clumsy magic, stoically translating word-for-word. The first two characters *Chaoxian* actually refer to the Korean minority in China, not to North Korea in particular. *Leng mian* simply means "cold noodles" but can be understood as "cold face" (since *mian* is also the character for "face"). A cold face describes someone with a grim expression. *Jia niu rou* does mean "to add beef" but for a dish which also existed in a vegetarian version, it indicates that this variety comes "with beef." A correct translation would be "Korean cold noodle soup with beef" or *Mul Naengmyeon*.

Shanghai (2015)

Shanghai (2015)

BELOW: *Jilie* definitely is the Chinese translation of the US razor brand. It is, however, also the phonetic transcription of "cutlet" which in turn goes back to the French original *côtelette,* a correct translation would be: Japanese Shrimp Cutlet.

Beijing (2010)

The more food the more the United States

Chengdu (2011)

Nanjing (2018)

COMMERCIALS
AND
PRODUCTS

With many commercials but also in shops and on products, such as clothes or stationery, English words have lost the original purpose of providing a meaningful translation of the Chinese original altogether and are used as purely ornamental elements to project an aura of internationality and worldliness. Notebooks and shirts leave Chinese out altogether.

Mianyang (2018)

Beijing (2011)

Beijing (2009)

Beijing (2010)

Shanghai (2018)

Beijing (2018)

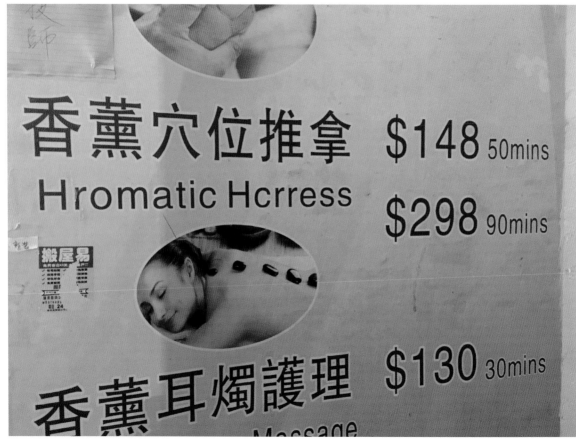

香薰穴位推拿 $148 50mins
Hromatic Hcrress
$298 90mins

香薰耳燭護理 $130 30mins
Massage

88

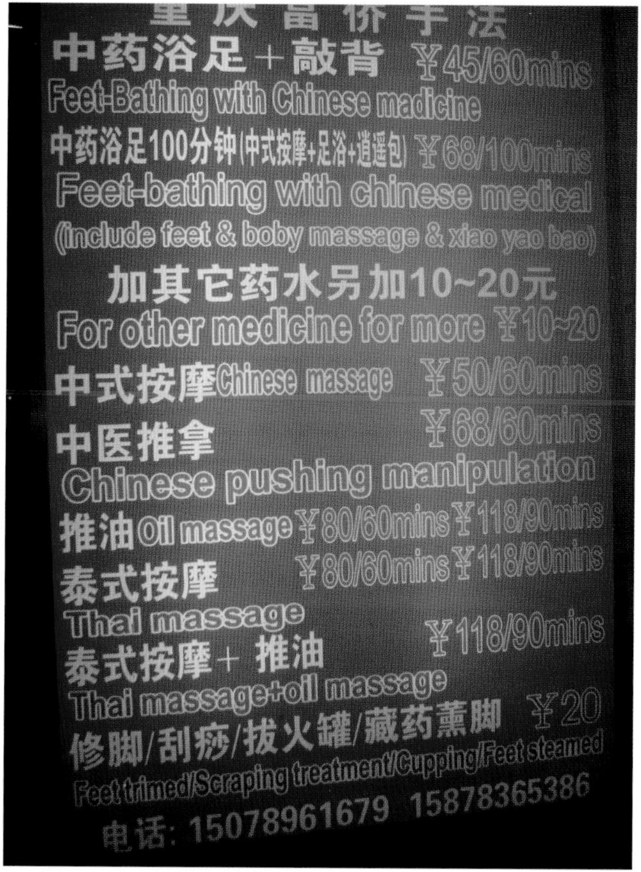

重庆当侨手法

中药浴足＋敲背 ￥45/60mins
Feet-Bathing with Chinese madicine

中药浴足100分钟(中式按摩+足浴+逍遥包) ￥68/100mins
Feet-bathing with chinese medical
(include feet & boby massage & xiao yao bao)

加其它药水另加10~20元
For other medicine for more ￥10~20

中式按摩 Chinese massage ￥50/60mins

中医推拿 ￥68/60mins
Chinese pushing manipulation

推油 Oil massage ￥80/60mins ￥118/90mins

泰式按摩 ￥80/60mins ￥118/90mins
Thai massage

泰式按摩＋推油 ￥118/90mins
Thai massage+oil massage

修脚/刮痧/拔火罐/藏药薰脚 ￥20
Feet trimed/Scraping treatment/Cupping/Feet steamed

电话: 15078961679 15878365386

Beijing (2009)

Xi'an (2016)

杨氏推拿 足道
MASSAGE
FOODO

Nanjing (2018)

Huai'an (2018)

Beijing (2015)

Beijing (2018)

Beijing (2018)

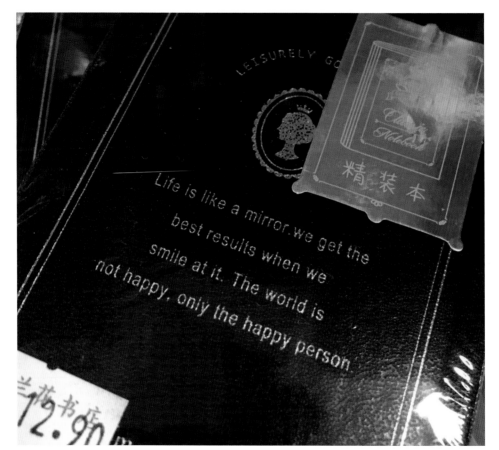

Beijing (2018)

Beijing (2018)

Beijing (2018)

Beijing (2012)

Beijing (2009)

IN PRAISE OF CHINGLISH

"Oliver Lutz Radtke's work on preserving and displaying Chinglish has been hugely important because it's captured an art form that is the result of a civilization that has developed faster than any other in the history of the planet. Someday, Chinglish may be gone from the earth, but we'll still have your work to point to and remember when China was scrambling and improvising its way to becoming a world power."

Rob Schmitz, Shanghai correspondent for National Public Radio and author of *Street of Eternal Happiness: Big City Dreams Along a Shanghai Road*

"Chinglish documents the struggle of mastering a foreign language. This struggle will go on, and at certain levels, there is nothing to be ashamed about when getting it wrong. It's the fascination of solving a riddle, because you automatically try to figure out what the right translation would have been. It's like watching someone slip on the banana peel of communication. Other peoples' falls and failures are funny, as long as no one really gets hurt."

Bernhard Bartsch, former China correspondent

"Chinglish illustrates the contrasts between the fundaments of the two languages, and in so doing it causes us to reflect on how those basic elements of the language might affect the way people in the two language zones might think in fundamentally different ways."

Kaiser Kuo, host of Sinica Podcast

"The prevalence of Chinglish in China at least demonstrates the people's willingness, if not the effort, to 'Westernize.' It's like watching little kids misusing words when learning their mother tongues. The earnestness in that effort is both funny and admirable."

Wu Hao, filmmaker, director of the critically acclaimed documentary *People's Republic of Desire*

"Chinglish makes me laugh. It also shows the Chinese openness to the world. How often do you see wrong Chinese translations in Germany? Hardly ever, which also stems from the fact that hardly anybody ever tries to make life in Germany easier for Chinese-speaking people. Chinglish, however, often results from the attempt to help English-speaking people to find their way in China. It shows the people's love and kindness towards strangers and guests."

Lea Deuber, China correspondent *Süddeutsche Zeitung*

"If the product of 'enjoying' Chinglish (and the equivalent laughter of Chinese people at foreigners mangling their tones or getting nonsensical tattoos) is laughter at the maddening intricacies of cross-cultural translation, something that in itself can be remedied, then it is potential common ground. As differences are increasingly exaggerated by political regimes in China and some western countries for political gain, common ground between people is going to become more difficult to find and more important to hold on to."

Jon Sullivan, Director of China Programs at the University of Nottingham Asia Research Institute

"I wouldn't call these examples Chinglish. Instead, I might call them good-will English. The original purpose was to help foreign tourists. Gradually, English becomes a ritual and a performance. It is like saying: See, we have English translations of our menu. We want to be helpful. We are modern. The precise meaning of the English translations becomes secondary."

Yang Guobin, Professor of Communication and Sociology at the University of Pennsylvania and author of *The Red Guard Generation and Political Activism in China*

"Chinglish will survive because communication must continue and because contexts are fluid. The idea of eradicating Chinglish is a fool's task, akin to the puritanical hubris of wanting to police 'proper' English and eradicate slang. Imagining a world without Chinglish means imagining a world without miscommunication."

David Bandurski, co-director of the China Media Project and author of *Dragons in Diamond Village*

"Chinglish is an erroneous translation as a result of ignorance or misconception, while intentional direct/literal translation can be an artistic choice that trades off idiomatic effect for cultural accent."

Xujun Eberlein, writer and author of *Apologies Forthcoming*

"Chinglish can be useful for improving intercultural communication if it generates shared laughter and discussion, perhaps best done by, when in a group, combining pointing out a particularly odd bit of Chinglish with asking those who are native speakers of Chinese what the funniest erroneous meaning from a flawed tone they've heard an English speaker make."

Jeffrey Wasserstrom, Chancellor's Professor of History at the University of California, Irvine, and co-author of *China in the 21st Century*

"You are doing a great contribution to raising people's awareness of the importance of doing the right kind of translation, how important it is, and how it should be done. It is a worthy cause and helps many people in Chinese who are trying to do the same thing. Keep it up and keep going."

Prof. Huang Youyi, Executive Vice President, Translators Association of China

"What you are doing is quite interesting and instructive."

Prof. Jiang Lu, Dean of School of European Studies at Beijing International Studies University

"Life is not just about economic growth. It is about cultures and mutual understanding. A discussion on Chinglish can help identify cultural differences and foster dialogue to clear up misunderstandings."

Liu Guosheng, CEO of China Tours and publisher

"I think, Chinglish is something of a linguistic borderland, innovative and surprising in many ways but also unpredictable. And, on a more practical level, it is part of traveling."

Lin Hierse, editor of sinonerds.com

"Please be the channel for making people understanding the Chinese mentality. Let people know that Chinese are making an effort to express themselves in English, even if it is not very accurate."

Shen Qilan, author and columnist

Beijing (2018)

PHOTO CREDITS

Bates, Diana: 86
Belle, Iris: 71 (right)
Bork, Henrik: 61
Carlaw, Anna: 24 (bottom right), 28, 60, 70, 71 (left), 92, 93
Christ, Judith: 88
Ding, Gang: 87
Eismann, Doreen: 47 (top left)
Eyssel, Benjamin: 18 (left)
Fan, Popo: 17 (top left)
Feldwisch-Drentrup, Hinnerk: 21, 52, 94 (left)
Fiederling, Johannes: 14, 16 (top right), 17 (top right), 53, 74 (top)
Göhring, Fabia: 13 (left), 40, 56
Göttlicher, Michael: 12

Hanson, Donna: 23, 36
Hildebrandt, Jens: 73
Kaspar, Ulrike: 19 (top)
Kaufmann, Matthias: 35
Kender, Kristian: 74 (bottom), 75 (right)
Khvastova, Marta: 63
Knorre, Dorothea: 39
Lingyan, Qian: 18 (right)
Linhard, Anna-Maria: 22 (right)
M. L.: 20 (right), 43, 58 (top)
Ott, Margus: 75 (left)
Porzycki, Marek: 46 (right)
Radunski, Michael: 22 (left)
Redl, Anke: 10 (left)
Scherbarth, Rico: 76 (left), 82
Schlichte, Johannes: 41
Schmitz, Rob: 76 (right), 77
Schünemann, Claudia: 80

Stolzenberg, Julia: 10 (right), 42 (left), 54
Strobel, Wesley: 20 (left), 29
Tsui, Jane: 24 (left), 45, 50
Weidel, Leonie: 46 (left), 94 (right)
Zhang, Yan: 24 (top right), 47 (bottom left), 103
Zhao, Weina: 68, 70, 72

All other photos credited to Oliver Lutz Radtke.

ACKNOWLEDGMENTS

First of all I would like to thank my editor, Katie Killebrew, at Gibbs Smith for making this third volume possible. It has been a pleasure, Katie. I would like to thank the following people for their insights and willingness to share their experiences and thoughts with me. They are all each in their own way important players in the field of international understanding and I feel privileged to know them: Huang Youyi, Jiang Lu, Xujun Eberlein, Liu Guosheng, Jon Sullivan, Jeffrey Wasserstrom, Bernhard Bartsch, Lea Deuber, Vincent Ni, Rob Schmitz, Kaiser Kuo, Yang Guobin, David Bandurski, Wu Hao, and Jay Wang. I would also like to thank all those that inspired my thinking in all kinds of ways and could not or did not want to be mentioned here.

I would especially like to thank David Moser for squeezing in time for our conversation. I thank Julia Sonntag for her critical mind.

Many thanks go to all photo contributors in this volume: Diana Bates, Iris Bell, Henrik Bork, Anna Carlaw, Judith Christ, Gang Ding, Doreen Eismann, Benjamin Eyssel, Popo Fan, Hinnerk Feldwisch-Drentrup, Johannes Fiederling, Fabia Göhring, Michael Göttlicher, Donna Hanson, Jens Hildebrandt, Ulrike Kaspar, Matthias Kaufmann, Kristian Kender, Marta Khvastova, Dorothea Knorre, Anna-Maria Linhard, M. L., Margus Ott, Marek Porzycki, Michael Radunski, Anke Redl, Rico Scherbarth, Johannes Schlichte, Rob Schmitz, Claudia Schünemann, Julia Stolzenberg, Wesley Strobel, Jane Tsui, Leonie Weidel, Yan Zhang, Weina Zhao. I feel I am in great company with you fellow collectors out there.

And last but not least, I would like to thank you, dear reader, who has shown interest in my work and in a topic that will continue to fascinate researchers and humble collectors such as myself.

Oliver Lutz Radtke
Palermo, Sicily, January 2019

About Chinglish Museum

Since 2000, author Oliver Lutz Radtke, a Chinese Studies major, a former journalist, and currently senior project manager for a major German foundation, has been collecting Chinglish examples from all over China. In order to preserve, display, and explain Chinglish for non-Chinese speakers, he founded www.chinglishmuseum.com. His goal is to make museum visitors interested in the intricacies of the Chinese language, the unexpected depths of translation issues, and celebrate linguistic diversity above everything else.

Want to keep up with the latest Chinglish discoveries?
Follow the author on social media at

 @chinglishmuseum

 chinglishmuseum